THE CALL OF THE WILD

At home in California, Buck has an easy, comfortable life. He is the biggest, strongest, most important dog in the place. He goes walking and swimming with the children, and he sits by his owner's fire in the winter.

But this is 1897, and dogs like Buck are needed in the Yukon, where men have found gold. So Buck is stolen from his home and taken north. There he learns how to pull a sled, traveling day after day over the frozen snow. He learns how to steal food, how to break the ice in water-holes, and how to fight the other dogs when they attack him. And he learns fast.

Soon Buck is one of the most famous sled-dogs in the north. But the north is a wild place, where the wolf howls to the moon and runs free in the forest. And the call of the wild comes to Buck in his dreams louder and louder . . .

OXFORD BOOKWORMS LIBRARY
Classics

The Call of the Wild

Stage 3 (1000 headwords)

Series Editor: Jennifer Bassett
Founder Editor: Tricia Hedge
Activities Editors: Jennifer Bassett and Alison Baxter

American Edition: Daphne Mackey, University of Washington

JACK LONDON

The Call of the Wild

Retold by
Nick Bullard

Illustrated by
Paul Fisher Johnson

OXFORD UNIVERSITY PRESS

OXFORD
UNIVERSITY PRESS

Great Clarendon Street, Oxford OX2 6DP

Oxford University Press is a department of the University of Oxford.
It furthers the University's objective of excellence in research, scholarship,
and education by publishing worldwide in

Oxford New York

Auckland Cape Town Dar es Salaam Hong Kong Karachi
Kuala Lumpur Madrid Melbourne Mexico City Nairobi
New Delhi Shanghai Taipei Toronto

With offices in

Argentina Austria Brazil Chile Czech Republic France Greece
Guatemala Hungary Italy Japan Poland Portugal Singapore
South Korea Switzerland Thailand Turkey Ukraine Vietnam

OXFORD and OXFORD ENGLISH are registered trade marks of
Oxford University Press in the UK and in certain other countries

This edition © Oxford University Press 2007

Database right Oxford University Press (maker)

First published in Oxford Bookworms 1995

4 6 8 10 9 7 5 3

ISBN 978 0 19 423752 9

Printed in Hong Kong

Map by: William Rowsell

CONTENTS

1

To the North

Buck did not read the newspapers. He did not know that trouble was coming for every big dog in California. Men had found gold in the Yukon, and these men wanted big, strong dogs to work in the cold and snow of the north.

Buck lived in Mr. Miller's big house in the sunny Santa Clara Valley. There were large gardens and fields of fruit trees around the house and a river nearby. In a big place like this, of course, there were many dogs. There were house dogs and farm dogs, but they were not important.

Buck lived in Mr. Miller's big house.

Buck was chief dog; he was born here, and this was his place. He was four years old and weighed a hundred and forty pounds. He went swimming with Mr. Miller's sons and walking with his daughters. He carried the grandchildren on his back, and he sat at Mr. Miller's feet in front of the fire in winter.

But this was 1897, and Buck did not know that men and dogs were hurrying to northwest Canada to look for gold. And he did not know that Manuel, one of Mr. Miller's gardeners, needed money for his large family. One day, when Mr. Miller was out, Manuel and Buck left the garden together. It was just an evening walk, Buck thought. No one saw them go, and only one man saw them arrive at the railway station. This man talked to Manuel and gave him some money. Then he tied a piece of rope around Buck's neck.

Buck growled, and he was surprised when the rope was pulled hard around his neck. He jumped at the man. The man caught him and suddenly Buck was on his back with his tongue out of his mouth. For a few moments he was unable to move, and it was easy for the two men to put him into the train.

When Buck woke up, the train was still moving. The man was sitting and watching him, but Buck was too quick for him, and he bit the man's hand hard. Then the rope was pulled again, and Buck had to let go.

That evening, the man took Buck to the back room of a bar in San Francisco. The barman looked at the man's hand and trousers covered in blood.

The man tied a piece of rope around Buck's neck.

"How much are they paying you for this?" he asked.

"I only get fifty dollars."

"And the man who stole him—how much did he get?" asked the barman.

"A hundred. He wouldn't take less."

"That makes a hundred and fifty. It's a good price for a dog like him. Here, help me to get him into this."

They took off Buck's rope and pushed him into a wooden box. He spent the night in the box in the back room of the bar. His neck still ached with pain from the rope, and he could not understand what it all meant. What did they want with him, these strange men? And where was Mr. Miller?

The next day Buck was carried in the box to the railway

3

station and put on a train to the north. For two days and nights the train traveled north, and for two days and nights Buck neither ate nor drank. Men on the train laughed at him and pushed sticks at him through the holes in the box. For two days and nights Buck got angrier, and hungrier, and thirstier. His eyes grew red, and he bit anything that moved.

In Seattle four men took Buck to a small, high-walled back garden, where a fat man in an old red coat was waiting. Buck was now very angry indeed, and he jumped and bit at the sides of his box. The fat man smiled and went to get an ax and a club.

"Are you going to take him out now?" asked one of the men.

"Of course," answered the fat man, and he began to break the box with his ax.

Immediately the four other men climbed up onto the wall to watch from a safe place.

As the fat man hit the box with his ax, Buck jumped at the sides, growling and biting, pulling with his teeth at the pieces of broken wood. After a few minutes there was a hole big enough for Buck to get out.

"Now, come here, red eyes," said the fat man, dropping his ax and taking the club in his right hand.

Buck jumped at the man, one hundred forty pounds of anger, his mouth wide open, ready to bite the man's neck. Just before his teeth touched the skin, the man hit him with the club. Buck fell to the ground. It was the first time anyone had hit him with a club, and he did not

The fat man dropped the ax and took the club in his right hand.

understand. He stood up and jumped again. Again the club hit him, and he crashed to the ground. Ten times he jumped at the man, and ten times the club hit him. Slowly he got to his feet, now only just able to stand. There was blood on his nose, mouth, and ears. Then the fat man walked up and hit him again, very hard, on the nose. The pain was terrible. Again, Buck jumped at the man, and again he was hit to the ground. A last time he jumped, and this time, when the man knocked him down, Buck did not move.

"He knows how to teach a dog a lesson," said one of the men on the wall. Then the four men jumped down and went back to the station.

"His name is Buck," said the fat man to himself, reading the letter that had come with the box. "Well, Buck, my boy," he said in a friendly voice, "we've argued a little, and I think the best thing to do now is to stop. Be a good dog, and we'll be friends. But if you're a bad dog, I'll have to use my club again. Understand?"

As he spoke, he touched Buck's head, and although Buck was angry inside, he did not move. When the man brought him water and meat, Buck drank and then ate the meat, piece by piece, from the man's hand.

Buck was beaten (he knew that), but he was not broken. He had learned that a man with a club was stronger than him. Every day he saw more dogs arrive, and each dog was beaten by the fat man. Buck understood that a man with a club must be obeyed, although he did not have to be a friend.

Men came to see the fat man and to look at the dogs. Sometimes they paid money and left with one or more of the dogs. One day a short, dark man came and looked at Buck.

"That's a good dog!" he cried. "How much do you want for him?"

"Three hundred dollars. It's a good price, Perrault," said the fat man.

Perrault smiled and agreed that it was a good price. He knew dogs, and he knew that Buck was an excellent dog. "One in ten thousand," Perrault said to himself.

Buck saw money put into the fat man's hand, and he was not surprised when he and another dog called Curly were taken away by Perrault. He took them to a ship, and later that day Buck and Curly stood and watched the coast get further and further away. They had seen the warm south for the last time.

Perrault took Buck and Curly down to the bottom of the ship. There they met another man, François. Perrault was a French-Canadian, but François was half-Indian, tall and dark. Buck learned quickly that Perrault and François were fair men, calm and honest. And they knew everything about dogs.

There were two other dogs on the ship. One was a big dog called Spitz, as white as snow. He was friendly to Buck at first, always smiling. He was smiling when he tried to steal Buck's food at the first meal. François was quick and hit Spitz before Buck had time to move. Buck decided that this was fair and began to like François a little.

Dave, the other dog, was not friendly. He wanted to be alone all the time. He ate, and slept, and was interested in nothing.

One day was very like another, but Buck noticed that the weather was getting colder. One morning, the ship's engines stopped, and there was a feeling of excitement in the ship. François leashed the dogs and took them outside. At the first step, Buck's feet went into something soft and white. He jumped back in surprise. The soft, white thing was also falling through the air, and it fell onto him. He tried to smell it, and then caught some on his tongue. It bit like fire and then disappeared. He tried again, and the same thing happened. People were watching him and laughing, and Buck felt ashamed, although he did not know why. It was his first snow.

It was his first snow.

2

The Law of Club and Tooth

Buck's first day at Dyea Beach was terrible. Every hour there was some new, frightening surprise. There was no peace, no rest—only continual noise and movement. And every minute there was danger, because these dogs and men were not town dogs and men. They knew only the law of club and tooth.

Buck had never seen dogs fight like these dogs; they were like wolves. In a few minutes he learned this from watching Curly. She tried to make friends with a dog, a big one, although not as big as she was. There was no warning. The dog jumped on Curly, his teeth closed together, then he jumped away, and Curly's face was torn open from eye to mouth.

Wolves fight like this, biting and jumping away, but the fight did not finish then. Thirty or forty more dogs ran up and made a circle around the fight, watching silently. Curly tried to attack the dog who had bitten her; he bit her a second time, and jumped away. When she attacked him again, he knocked her backwards, and she fell on the ground. She never stood up again, because this was what the other dogs were waiting for. They moved in, and in a moment she was under a crowd of dogs.

It was all very sudden. Buck saw Spitz run out from the crowd with his tongue out of his mouth, laughing. Then he saw François with an ax and two or three other men with clubs jump in among the dogs. Two minutes later the last of the dogs was chased away. But Curly lay dead in the snow, her body torn almost to pieces. Curly's death often came back to Buck in his dreams. He understood that once a dog was down on the ground, he was dead. He also remembered Spitz laughing, and from that moment he hated him.

Then Buck had another surprise. François put a harness on him. Buck had seen harnesses on horses, and now he was made to work like a horse, pulling François on a sled into the forest and returning with wood for the fire. Buck worked with Spitz and Dave. The two other dogs had worked in a harness before, and Buck learned by watching them. He also learned to stop and turn when François shouted.

"Those three are very good dogs," François told Perrault. "That Buck pulls very well, and he's learning quickly."

Perrault had important letters and official papers to take to Dawson City, so that afternoon he bought two more dogs, two brothers called Billee and Joe. Billee was very friendly, but Joe was the opposite. In the evening Perrault bought one more dog, an old dog with one eye. His name was Sol-leks, which means The Angry One. Like Dave, he made no friends; all he wanted was to be alone.

That night Buck discovered another problem. Where was he going to sleep? François and Perrault were in their tent, but when he went in, they shouted angrily and threw things at him. Outside it was very cold and windy. He lay

Buck worked like a horse, pulling François on a sled.

down in the snow, but he was too cold to sleep.

He walked around the tents trying to find the other dogs. But, to his surprise, they had disappeared. He walked around Perrault's tent, very, very cold, wondering what to do. Suddenly, the snow under his feet fell in, and he felt something move. He jumped back, waiting for the attack, but heard only a friendly bark. There, in a warm hole under the snow, was Billee.

So that was what you had to do. Buck chose a place, dug himself a hole, and in a minute he was warm and asleep. He slept well, although his dreams were bad.

When he woke up, at first he did not know where he was. It had snowed in the night, and the snow now lay thick and heavy above him. Suddenly he was afraid—the fear of a wild animal when it is caught and cannot escape. Growling, he threw himself at the snow, and a moment later, he had jumped upwards into the daylight. He saw the tents and remembered everything, from the time he had gone for a walk with Manuel to the moment he had dug the hole the night before.

Buck jumped upwards into the daylight.

"What did I say?" shouted François to Perrault, when he saw Buck come up out of the snow. "That Buck learns quickly."

Perrault smiled slowly. He was carrying important papers, and he needed good dogs. He was very pleased to have Buck.

They bought three more dogs that morning, and a quarter of an hour later all nine dogs were in harness and on their way up the Dyea Canyon. Buck was not sorry to be moving, and although it was hard work, he almost enjoyed it. He was also surprised to see that Dave and Sol-leks no longer looked bored and miserable. Pulling in a harness was their job, and they were happy to do it.

Dave was sled-dog, the dog nearest to the sled. In front of him was Buck, then came Sol-leks. In front of them were the six other dogs, with Spitz as leader at the front. François had put Buck between Dave and Sol-leks because they could teach him the work. Buck learned well, and they were good teachers. When Buck pulled the wrong way, Dave always bit his leg, but only lightly. Once, when they stopped, Buck got tied up in his harness, and it took ten minutes to get started again. Both Dave and Sol-leks gave him a good beating for that mistake. Buck understood and was more careful after that.

It was a hard day's journey, up the Dyea Canyon and into the mountains. They camped that night at Lake Bennett. Here there were thousands of gold miners. They were building boats to sail up the lake when the ice melted in the spring. Buck made his hole in the snow and slept well, but was woken up very early and harnessed to the sled. The first day they had traveled on snow that had been

They camped that night at Lake Bennett.

hardened by many sleds, and they covered forty miles. But the next day, and for days afterwards, they were on new snow. The work was harder, and they went slowly. Usually, Perrault went in front, on snowshoes, flattening the snow a little for the dogs. François stayed by the sled. Sometimes the two men changed places, but there were many small lakes and rivers, and Perrault understood ice better. He always knew when the ice across a river was very thin.

Day after day Buck pulled in his harness. They started in the morning before it was light, and they stopped in the evening after dark, ate a piece of fish, and went to sleep in their holes under the snow. Buck was always hungry. François gave him a pound and a half of dried fish a day, and it was never enough. The other dogs were given only a pound; they were smaller and could stay alive on less food.

Buck learned to eat quickly; if he was too slow, the other dogs stole his food. He saw Pike, one of the new dogs, steal some meat from the sled when Perrault wasn't looking. The next day Buck stole some and got away unseen. Perrault was very angry, but he thought another dog, Dub, had taken it and so punished him instead of Buck.

Buck was learning how to live in the north. In the south he had never stolen, but there he had never been so hungry. He stole cleverly and secretly, remembering the beatings from the man with the club. Buck was learning the law of club and tooth.

He learned to eat any food—anything that he could get his teeth into. He learned to break the ice on water holes with his feet when he wanted to drink. He was stronger, harder, and could see and smell better than ever before. In a way, he was remembering back to the days when wild dogs traveled in packs through the forest, killing for meat as they went. It was easy for him to learn to fight like a wolf, because it was in his blood. In the evenings, when he pointed his nose at the moon and howled long and loud, he was remembering the dogs and wolves that had come before him.

3

The Wild Animal

The wild animal was strong in Buck, and as he traveled across the snow, it grew stronger and stronger. And as Buck grew stronger, he hated Spitz more and more, although he was careful never to start a fight.

But Spitz was always showing his teeth to Buck, trying to start a fight. And Buck knew that if he and Spitz fought, one of them would die.

The fight almost happened one night when they stopped by Lake Laberge. There was heavy snow, and it was very cold. The lake was frozen, and François, Perrault, and the dogs had to spend the night on the ice, under a big rock. Buck had made a warm hole in the snow and was sorry to leave it to get his piece of fish. But when he had eaten and returned to his hole, he found Spitz in it. Buck had tried

The lake was frozen, and they spent the night on the ice.

not to fight Spitz before, but this was too much. He attacked him angrily. Spitz was surprised. He knew Buck was big, but he didn't know he was so wild. François was surprised too, and guessed why Buck was angry.

"Go on Buck!" he shouted. "Fight him, the dirty thief!"

Spitz was also ready to fight, and the two dogs circled one another, looking for the chance to jump in. But suddenly there was a shout from Perrault, and they saw eighty or a hundred dogs around the sled. The dogs came from an Indian village, and they were searching for the food that they could smell on the sled. Perrault and François tried to fight them off with their clubs, but the dogs, made crazy by the smell of the food, showed their teeth and fought back.

Buck had never seen dogs like these. They were all skin and bone, but hunger made them fight like wild things. Three of them attacked Buck, and in seconds his head and legs were badly bitten. Dave and Sol-leks stood side by side, covered in blood, fighting bravely. Joe and Pike jumped on one dog, and Pike broke its neck with one bite. Buck caught another dog by the neck and tasted blood. He threw himself on the next one, and then felt teeth in his own neck. It was Spitz, attacking him from the side.

Perrault and François came to help with clubs, but then they had to run back to save the food. It was safer for the nine sled-dogs to run away across the lake. Several of them were badly hurt, and they spent an unhappy night hiding among the trees.

At first light they returned to the sled and found Perrault and François tired and angry. Half their food was gone. The Indian dogs had even eaten one of Perrault's shoes. François looked at his dogs unhappily.

"Ah, my friends," he said softly, "perhaps those bites will make you ill. What do you think, Perrault?"

Perrault said nothing. They still had four hundred miles to travel, and he hoped very much that his sled-dogs had not caught rabies from the Indian dogs.

The harness was torn and damaged, and it was two hours before they were moving, traveling slowly and painfully over the most difficult country that they had been in.

The Thirty Mile River was not frozen. It ran too fast to freeze. They spent six days trying to find a place to cross, and every step was dangerous for dogs and men. Twelve times they found ice bridges across the river, and Perrault walked carefully onto them, holding a long piece of wood. And twelve times he fell through a bridge and was saved by the piece of wood, which caught on the sides of the hole. But the temperature was 45° below zero, and each time Perrault fell into the water, he had to light a fire to dry and warm himself. Once, the sled fell through the ice, with Dave and Buck, and they were covered in ice by the time Perrault and François pulled them out of the river. Again, a fire was needed to save them. Another time, Spitz and the dogs in front fell through the ice—Buck and Dave and François at the sled had to pull backwards. That day they traveled only a quarter of a mile.

When they got to the Hootalinqua and good ice, Buck and the other dogs were very, very tired. But they were late, so Perrault made them run faster. In three days they went a hundred and ten miles and reached the Five Fingers.

The other dogs had hard feet from years of pulling sleds, but Buck's feet were still soft from his easy life down south. All day he ran painfully, and when they camped for the night, he lay down like a dead dog. He was hungry, but he was too tired to walk to the fish, so François brought it to him. One day François made four little shoes for him, and this made Buck much more comfortable. François forgot the shoes one morning, and Buck refused to move. He lay on his back with his feet in the air until François put the shoes on. Later his feet grew harder, and the shoes were not needed.

One morning, at the Pelly River, a dog called Dolly went suddenly mad. She howled long and loud like a wolf and then jumped at Buck. Buck ran, with Dolly one step behind him. She could not catch him, but he could not escape from her. They ran half a mile, and then Buck heard François call to him. He turned and ran towards the man, sure that François would save him. François stood, holding his ax, and as Buck passed, the ax crashed down on Dolly's head.

Buck fell down by the sled, too tired to move. Immediately, Spitz attacked him and bit his helpless enemy twice, as hard as he could. But François saw this and gave Spitz a terrible beating for it.

Buck lay on his back until François put the shoes on.

"He's a wild dog, that Spitz," said Perrault. "One day he'll kill Buck."

"Buck is wilder," replied François. "I've been watching him. One day he'll get very angry, and he'll fight Spitz; and he'll win."

François was right. Buck wanted to be lead-dog. Spitz knew this and hated him. Buck started to help the other dogs when Spitz punished them for being lazy. One morning, Pike refused to get up, and Spitz looked for him everywhere. When he found him, he jumped at him. But suddenly, Buck attacked Spitz. The other dogs saw this, and it became more and more difficult for Spitz to lead them. But the days passed without a chance for a fight, and soon they were pulling into Dawson City on a cold gray afternoon.

They stayed in Dawson for seven days. When they left, Perrault was carrying some more very important papers, and he wanted to travel back as fast as possible.

They traveled fifty miles the first day and the same the second. But it was difficult work for François. Buck and Spitz hated each other, and the other dogs were not afraid of Spitz any more. One night Pike stole half a fish from Spitz and ate it standing next to Buck. And every time Buck went near Spitz, he growled and the hair on his back stood up angrily. The other dogs fought in their harnesses, and François often had to stop the sled. He knew that Buck was the problem, but Buck was too clever for him, and François never saw him actually starting a fight.

One night in camp, the dogs saw a snow rabbit, and in a second they were all chasing it, with Spitz in front. Nearby was another camp, with fifty dogs, who also joined the chase. The rabbit was running fast on top of the snow, but the snow was soft, and it was more difficult for the dogs. When Spitz caught the rabbit, throwing it in the air with his teeth, Buck was just behind. Spitz stopped, and Buck hit him, very hard. The two dogs fell in the snow. Spitz bit Buck very quickly, twice, and then jumped away, watching carefully.

The time had come, and Buck knew that either he or Spitz must die. They watched one another, circling slowly. The moon was shining brightly on the snow, and in the cold still air not a leaf moved on the trees. The other dogs finished eating the rabbit and then turned to watch.

Spitz caught the rabbit, throwing it in the air.

Spitz was a good fighter. He was full of hate and anger, but he was also intelligent. Every time Buck tried to bite his throat, he met Spitz's own teeth. Then, each time Buck attacked, Spitz moved and bit him on the side as he passed. After a few minutes, Buck was covered in blood. He attacked again, but this time turned at the last minute and went under Spitz, biting his left front leg. The bone broke, and Spitz was standing on three legs. Buck tried to knock Spitz down and then repeated his earlier attack. He broke Spitz's right front leg.

There was no hope for Spitz now. Buck got ready for his final attack, while the circle of sixty dogs watched and crowded nearer and nearer, waiting for the end. At last Buck jumped, in and out, and Spitz went down in the snow. A second later the waiting pack was on top of him, and Spitz had disappeared. Buck stood and watched. The wild animal had made its kill.

4

The New Lead-dog

"**W**ell, what did I say? Buck's a real fighter, all right," said François the next morning when he discovered that Spitz had disappeared and that Buck was covered in blood.

"Spitz fought like a wolf," said Perrault, as he looked at the bites all over Buck.

"And Buck fought like ten wolves," answered François. "And we'll travel faster now. No more Spitz, no more trouble."

François started to harness the dogs. He needed a new lead-dog, and decided that Sol-leks was the best dog that he had. But Buck jumped at Sol-leks and took his place.

"Look at Buck!" said François, laughing. "He's killed Spitz, and now he wants to be lead-dog. Go away, Buck!"

He pulled Buck away and tried to harness Sol-leks again. Sol-leks was unhappy too. He was frightened of Buck, and when François turned his back, Buck took Sol-leks' place again. Now François was angry.

"I'll show you!" he cried, and went to get a heavy club from the sled.

Buck remembered the man in the red coat and moved away. This time, when Sol-leks was harnessed as lead-dog, Buck did not try to move in. He kept a few feet away and circled around François carefully. But when François called him to his old place in front of Dave, Buck refused. He had won his fight with Spitz, and he wanted to be lead-dog.

For an hour the two men tried to harness him. Buck did not run away, but he did not let them catch him. Finally, François sat down, and Perrault looked at his watch. It was getting late. The two men looked at one another and smiled. François walked up to Sol-leks, took off his harness, led him back, and harnessed him in his old place. Then he called Buck. All the other dogs were harnessed, and the only empty place was now the one at the front. But Buck did not move.

"Put down the club," said Perrault.

François dropped the club, and immediately Buck came up to the front of the team. François harnessed him, and in a minute the sled was moving.

Buck was an excellent leader. He moved and thought quickly and led the other dogs well. A new leader made no

The only empty place was the one at the front.

25

difference to Dave and Sol-leks; they continued to pull hard. But the other dogs had had an easy life when Spitz was leading. They were surprised when Buck made them work hard and punished them for their mistakes. Pike, the second dog, was usually lazy, but by the end of the first day he was pulling harder than he had ever pulled in his life. The first night in camp Buck fought Joe, another difficult dog, and after that there were no more problems with him. The team started to pull together and to move faster and faster.

"I've never seen a dog like Buck!" cried François. "Never! He's worth a thousand dollars. What do you think, Perrault?"

Perrault agreed. They were moving quickly and covering more ground every day. The snow was good and hard, and no new snow fell. The temperature dropped to 45° below zero and didn't change.

This time there was more ice on the Thirty Mile River, and they crossed in a day. Some days they ran fifty miles, or even more. They reached Skagway in fourteen days, the fastest time ever.

For three days the dogs rested in Skagway. Then François put his arms around Buck's neck and said goodbye to him. And that was the last of François and Perrault. Like other men, they passed out of Buck's life for ever.

Two new men took Buck and his team back north on the long journey to Dawson, traveling with several other dog-teams. It was heavy work; the sled was loaded with letters for the gold miners of Dawson. Buck did not like it,

It was heavy work; the sled was loaded with letters.

but he worked hard and made the other dogs work hard, too. Each day was the same. They started early, before it was light, and at night they stopped and camped, and the dogs ate. For the dogs this was the best part of the day, first eating, and then resting by the fire.

Buck liked to lie by the fire, looking at the burning wood. Sometimes he thought about Mr. Miller's house in California. More often he remembered the man in the red coat and his club, the death of Curly, the fight with Spitz, and the good things that he had eaten. But sometimes he remembered other things. These were things that he remembered through his parents, and his parents' parents, and all the dogs which had lived before him.

Sometimes as he lay there, he seemed to see, in a waking dream, a different fire. And he saw next to him, not the Indian cook, but another man, a man with shorter legs and longer arms. This man had long hair and deep eyes, and he made strange noises in his throat. He was very frightened of the dark and looked around him all the time, holding a heavy stone in his hand. He wore the skin of an animal on his back, and Buck could see thick hair all over his body.

Buck sat by the fire with this hairy man, and in the circling darkness beyond the fire he could see many eyes—the eyes of hungry animals waiting to attack. And he growled softly in his dream until the Indian cook shouted, "Hey, Buck, wake up!" Then the strange world disappeared, and Buck's eyes saw the real fire again.

When they reached Dawson, the dogs were tired and needed a week's rest. But in two days they were moving south again, with another heavy load of letters. Both dogs and men were unhappy. It snowed every day as well, and on soft new snow it was harder work pulling the sleds.

The men took good care of their dogs. In the evenings, the dogs ate first, the men second, and they always checked the dogs' feet before they slept. But every day the dogs became weaker. Buck had pulled sleds for eighteen hundred miles that winter, and he was as tired as the others.

But Dave was not only tired; he was ill. Every evening he lay down the minute after the sled stopped and did not stand up until morning. The men looked at him, but they could find no broken bones. Something was wrong inside.

Buck sat by the fire with this hairy man.

One day he started to fall down while in his harness. The sled stopped, and the driver took him out of his harness. He wanted to give him a rest and let him run free behind the sled. But Dave did not want to stop working. He hated to see another dog doing his work, so he ran along beside the sled, trying to push Sol-leks out of his place. When the sled made its next stop, Dave bit through Solleks' harness and pushed him away. Then he stood there, in his old place in front of the sled, waiting for his harness and the order to start pulling.

The driver decided it was kinder to let him work. Dave pulled all day, but the next morning he was too weak to move. The driver harnessed up without Dave, and drove a few hundred feet. Then he stopped, took his gun, and walked back. The dogs heard a shot, and then the man came quickly back. The sled started to move again, but Buck knew, and every dog knew, what had happened.

5
More Hard Work

T hirty days after leaving Dawson City, the team arrived back in Skagway. They were very, very tired. Buck now weighed only a hundred and fifteen pounds, and the other dogs were also very thin.

They were not ill; they just needed a long, long rest. But at Skagway there were mountains of letters waiting to go north, so the men had to buy new, strong dogs. The old ones, now useless for work, were sold.

Two American men, called Hal and Charles, bought Buck and his team, together with the harness. Charles was forty years old, with light hair and watery blue eyes. Hal was a young man of twenty with a big shiny gun and a big knife in his belt. These things, more than anything, showed how young he was. Both men were clearly new to the north, and its hard and dangerous life.

They took the dogs back to their untidy camp, where a woman was waiting. This was Mercedes—Charles's wife and Hal's sister.

Buck watched the men take down the tent and load all their luggage on the sled. They didn't know how to do it sensibly, and every time they put something on the sled, Mercedes moved it. Often they had to take things off the sled and start again.

Three men came up and watched, laughing.

Two American men bought Buck and his team.

"You've got a heavy load on that sled," said one of them. "Why don't you leave the tent here in Skagway?"

"How could we live without a tent?" asked Mercedes, throwing up her hands in the air.

"It's spring now. You won't have any more cold weather."

"I have to have a tent," she answered, and she helped Charles and Hal with the last few boxes.

"Do you think that load will stay on?" asked another man.

"Why shouldn't it?" asked Charles.

"Well, it's a bit heavy on top. Do you think your dogs will be able to pull that?"

"Of course they will," said Hal. The sled was now ready to go. "Come on, dogs, pull!" he shouted.

The dogs pulled as hard as they could, but the sled did not move.

"The lazy animals!" shouted Hal, picking up his whip.

But Mercedes stopped him. "Oh, Hal, you mustn't," she cried, pulling the whip away from him. "The poor dogs. You must promise to be nice to them, or I'm staying here!"

"You know nothing about dogs," answered Hal. "Leave me alone. Dogs are lazy, and you have to whip them. Everybody knows that. Ask those men if you don't believe me."

Mercedes turned and looked at the watching men.

"They're tired, if you really want to know," said one of them. "They've been working very hard, and they need a rest."

"Rest?" laughed Hal. "These stupid dogs are just lazy."

Now Mercedes decided that her brother was right. "Don't listen to that man," she said. "You're driving our dogs, and you do what you think is best."

Now Hal used his whip on the dogs. They pulled and pulled, but the sled stayed where it was. Hal was still using his whip when Mercedes stopped him again and put her arms around Buck.

"You poor, poor dears," she said. "Why don't you pull hard?—then nobody will whip you."

One of the men watching now spoke again. "I don't care what happens to you," he said, "but I'm sorry for the dogs. The sled is frozen to the snow, and you'll have to break it out. Push it from one side to the other to break the ice."

Hal tried again, but this time he broke the ice under the sled. The heavy sled started to move slowly, with Buck and

Now Hal used his whip on the dogs.

his team pulling hard under the whip. After a hundred yards they had to turn into another street. It was a difficult turn with a top-heavy load, and Hal was not a good driver. As they turned, the sled went over onto its side, throwing boxes and packets into the street. The dogs didn't stop. The sled was not so heavy now, and they pulled it easily on its side. The whip had made them angry, and they started to run. Hal cried "Stop!" but the dogs continued through Skagway, and the rest of the luggage fell off as they ran.

People helped to catch the dogs and to pick up all the things from the street. They also told the men that if they wanted to reach Dawson, they needed twice as many dogs and half as much luggage. Hal and Charles went back to the camp and started to look at the luggage and throw things away. Tent, blankets, and plates were taken out. Mercedes cried when most of her clothes went. When they had finished, Mercedes was still crying, there was a lot of luggage on the road, and there was still a lot to go on the sled.

Then Charles and Hal went out and bought six more dogs, so they now had fourteen. But the new dogs were not real sled-dogs, and they knew nothing about the work. Charles and Hal put them into harness, but Buck could not teach them how to pull a sled. So now there were six dogs who couldn't pull at all, and eight who were tired after pulling for twenty-five hundred miles. But Charles and Hal were happy. They had more dogs than any sled that they had seen at Skagway. They didn't know that no sled could carry enough food for fourteen dogs.

The next morning Buck led the team up the street. They moved slowly, because they were tired before they started. Buck had pulled to Dawson and back twice, and he didn't want to do it again. He had watched Hal and Charles and Mercedes, and he saw that they didn't know how to do anything. And, as the days passed, he saw that they could not learn. It took them half the evening to get everything ready for the night—and it took them half the morning to get ready to leave. And when they did start, they often had to stop because something had fallen off the sled. On some days they traveled twenty miles and on some days only ten.

They didn't have enough dog food when they started, and they used what they had much too quickly. Hal gave the dogs extra food because he wanted them to pull harder. Mercedes gave them extra food because she was sorry for them. But it was not food that they wanted, but rest.

Soon Hal saw that they had traveled only a quarter of the way to Dawson, but had eaten half their food. He had to give the dogs less food. It was easy to give them less food, but it was impossible to make them travel faster.

Dub had pulled hard and well all the way from Skagway, but he had hurt his leg. It got worse and worse until finally Hal had to shoot him. The six new dogs, now weak and ill from hunger and hard work, died next.

Hal, Charles, and Mercedes had started the journey happily; but now they were tired, angry, and miserable. Charles and Hal argued about everything, because each thought that he was working harder than the other. And Mercedes was unhappy because she thought that she shouldn't have to work. She was tired, so she rode on the sled, making the work even harder for the dogs. She rode for days, until the dogs could not move the sled. The men asked her to walk, but she would not leave the sled. One day they lifted her off. She sat in the snow and did not move. They went off with the sled and traveled three miles. Then they turned, went back, and lifted her on again.

Buck and the other dogs were now just skin and bone. They pulled when they could, and when they couldn't, they

Mercedes sat in the snow and did not move.

lay down in the snow. When they were whipped, they stood up and tried to pull again.

One day Billee fell and could not stand up. Hal killed him and threw him into the snow. Buck and the other dogs knew that soon they were going to die, too. On the next day Koona died, and there were only five dogs left: Joe, Pike, Sol-leks the one-eyed, Teek, and Buck.

It was beautiful spring weather. The snow and ice were melting, the plants were growing, and the forest animals were waking from their winter sleep. It was a lovely morning when the two men, and the five dogs pulling Mercedes on the sled, came into John Thornton's camp at White River. They stopped, and the dogs dropped down immediately to rest.

John Thornton was mending an ax, and he went on working as he talked to Hal.

"Is it safe to cross the river here?" asked Hal.

"No, the ice is too thin. It's much too dangerous," answered Thornton.

"People have told us that before," laughed Hal, "but we got here with no problems."

"Only somebody very stupid would cross the White River here," said Thornton.

"That's what you think," said Hal. "But we've got to get to Dawson." He picked up his whip. "Come on, Buck! Get up now! Let's go!"

Thornton went on working. He had warned them, but he knew he couldn't stop these stupid men from going on.

But Buck didn't get up. Sol-leks stood up slowly, then Teek and Joe, and finally Pike. But Buck stayed where he was. The whip came down on him again and again. Thornton started to speak, then stopped, and began to walk up and down.

Hal now put down his whip, and started to hit Buck with a club. But Buck had decided not to get up. He had felt thin ice under his feet all day and he saw thin ice in front of him. The club hit him again and again, but Buck felt almost nothing.

Then suddenly, with a wild cry, John Thornton jumped on Hal, throwing him backwards. Mercedes screamed.

"If you hit that dog again, I'll kill you," Thornton shouted.

"He's my dog," Hal replied. There was blood on his face. "Get out of my way, or I'll hit you, too. I'm going to Dawson."

Thornton stood between Hal and Buck and did not move. Hal took out his long knife, but Thornton knocked it out of his hand. Mercedes screamed again. Then Thornton picked up Hal's knife and cut Buck out of the harness.

Hal didn't want to fight, and Buck was not worth fighting for; he was nearly dead. Hal started the sled and went down towards the river. Buck lifted his head and watched the sled move away. Pike was leading, and Joe, Teek and Sol-leks were behind him. Hal was walking in front of the sled and Mercedes was riding on it; Charles was walking behind.

As Buck watched, Thornton felt his body with gentle hands, searching for broken bones. Buck was very thin, very tired, and very weak, but Thornton didn't think he was going to die. Then both dog and man watched the sled as it went slowly out on to the ice in the middle of the river. Suddenly the back of the sled went down, and the front went up into the air. Mercedes screamed, and Charles turned and took one step back. Then a big piece of ice broke off, and dogs, sled, and people disappeared; there was only a big hole in the ice.

John Thornton and Buck looked at one another.

"You poor thing," said John Thornton, and Buck licked his hand.

"You poor thing," said John Thornton, *and Buck licked his hand.*

6

For the Love of a Man

John Thornton had been ill in December, and his two friends had had to leave him at White River and go on to Dawson. They left him in the camp with plenty of food, and with his two dogs, Skeet and Blackie. Now the spring had come, and he was almost well. He lay in the sun by the river with Buck, watching the water and listening to the birds, slowly getting stronger and stronger.

A rest is very welcome after running three thousand miles, and Buck slowly got fatter and stronger. It was a peaceful, lazy time for both man and dogs while they waited for Thornton's friends to return from Dawson.

He lay in the sun by the river with Buck.

Skeet made friends with Buck immediately, and while Buck was still very ill, every morning she washed his cuts carefully with her tongue. Blackie, too, was friendly, and as Buck grew stronger, the three dogs often played games together. Sometimes Thornton joined the games too.

The days passed very happily, and for the first time, Buck learned to love. He had never loved a man before. He and Mr. Miller in the Santa Clara valley had been very good friends, but Buck had not loved him. John Thornton had saved his life, but he was also a man who was naturally kind to animals. He took very good care of his dogs, not because it was sensible to do that, but because he felt they were his children. He was always talking to Buck, holding his head, and shaking it lovingly. In answer, Buck liked to take Thornton's hand gently in his mouth.

Buck was happy to lie on the ground all day and watch Thornton. And when Thornton spoke to him or touched him, Buck went wild with happiness. At first, he was afraid that Thornton was going to disappear, like Perrault and François, and at night he sometimes woke up and went to the tent to make sure that he was still there.

But something was changing in Buck. He had lived in the north a long time now, and he was almost a wild dog. He was happy to sit by Thornton's fire, but he sat as a wild animal, and his dreams were filled with other animals— dogs, half-wolves, and wild wolves. They seemed to call him into the forest, and sometimes Buck wanted to leave the fire and answer the call. But every time he went into the trees, his love for Thornton brought him back.

It was only Thornton who stopped him going into the forest. Other men did not interest him. Visitors to the camp tried to make friends with him, but Buck stayed cold. When Thornton's two friends, Hans and Pete, arrived from Dawson, Buck refused to notice them at first. Then he saw that they were friends of Thornton's, and after that he accepted them; but they were not his friends. They were, like Thornton, kind men, and they understood that Buck loved Thornton, and him alone.

Thornton, too, understood Buck. One day, Buck and the three men were sitting on some high rocks, three hundred feet above the river. Thornton wondered if Buck would obey any order, even a crazy one. "Jump, Buck!" he shouted, pointing down to the river. A second later the three men were holding Buck back as he tried to jump.

"That was very strange," said Pete, when they had sat down again.

"Not strange—wonderful," said Thornton. "Terrible, too. Sometimes it frightens me."

"Yes. I feel sorry for any man who hits you when Buck's near," said Pete.

"So do I," said Hans.

It happened in the autumn in Circle City. A man called Burton was starting a fight with another man in a bar. Thornton stepped between them to try to stop them. Buck was, as usual, lying in the corner watching. Burton hit Thornton, and he nearly fell, just catching a table. Buck flew through the air at Burton's throat. Burton saved his life by putting up his arm, and was thrown on to the ground, with Buck on top of him. Buck took his teeth out of the man's arm and this time bit into his throat. Then a crowd of people pulled Buck off, and a doctor was called. Everyone agreed that Buck had only attacked because he saw Thornton in danger, and from that day Buck's name became famous all over the north.

Later that year, Buck saved Thornton in a different way. The three men were taking a boat down a fast and rocky river. Thornton was in the boat, while Hans and Pete moved along the river bank, holding the boat with a rope. Buck followed them, keeping a worried eye on Thornton.

Thornton was in the boat, while Hans and Pete moved along the river bank.

43

They came to a more dangerous part of the river, and the boat started to go too quickly. Hans pulled on the rope to stop it, and pulled too hard. The boat turned over, and Thornton was thrown into the water and carried down river towards rocks where no swimmer could live.

Buck jumped in immediately and swam three hundred yards until he reached Thornton. Then he turned, and with Thornton holding his tail, Buck swam towards the river bank. But they moved slowly, and all the time the river was carrying them towards the place where the water crashed six feet down onto rocks. Thornton knew that they would not get to the bank quickly enough, so he let go of Buck, held on to a rock in the middle of the water, and shouted, "Go, Buck, go!"

Buck swam as hard as he could to the bank, and Pete and Hans pulled him out.

It was hard for Thornton to hold on to his rock in that wild water, and his friends knew they had only a few minutes to save him. They tied their rope around Buck, who at once jumped into the river and tried to swim to Thornton. The first time, the water took him past the rock, and Pete and Hans had to pull him back. The second time, he swam higher up the river, and the water brought him down to Thornton. Thornton held on to Buck, and Hans and Pete pulled the rope as hard as they could. Man and dog disappeared under the water, banging into rocks, turning over and over, sometimes with Buck on top, sometimes Thornton. When Hans and Pete finally pulled

Thornton held on to Buck.

them out, both seemed more dead than alive. But after a while their eyes opened, and life returned.

That winter, at Dawson, Buck did something that made him even more famous in the north. It was also very helpful to the three men. They wanted to make a journey to look for gold in the east, and they needed money. They were in a bar one day when some of the men started to talk about dogs. One man said that he had a dog who was strong enough to pull a sled with five hundred pounds on it. Another said his dog could pull six hundred. A third man, called Matthewson, said his dog could pull seven hundred pounds.

"That's nothing," said Thornton. "Buck can pull a thousand."

"Can he break the sled out when it's frozen to the ice and then start it moving? And pull it a hundred yards?" asked Matthewson.

"He can break it out, and start it, and pull it a hundred yards," said Thornton.

"Well," said Matthewson, speaking slowly and loudly. "I've got a thousand dollars here, and I say he can't." As he spoke, he took a bag of gold and put it down on the table.

Suddenly Thornton was worried. He knew Buck was strong, but was he strong enough? Now ten men were watching him and waiting. He didn't have a thousand dollars, and neither did Hans or Pete.

"I've got a sled outside with a thousand pounds on it," said Matthewson. "So it's easy if you want to try."

Thornton didn't know what to say. He looked at the other men in the bar. One of them was an old friend, Jim O'Brien.

"Can you lend me a thousand dollars, Jim?" he asked softly.

"Sure," said O'Brien, putting another bag of gold next to Matthewson's. "But I don't think the dog can do it, John."

Everybody went out into the street. There were two or three hundred men around Matthewson's sled. The sled had been outside the bar for two hours, and it was frozen to the ice, in a temperature of 50° below zero. Most of the men thought that Buck was not strong enough, and Matthewson smiled happily.

"Shall we make it two thousand dollars?" he asked.

Thornton, Hans, and Pete talked for a minute. They had only four hundred dollars, but they added this to O'Brien's thousand. Matthewson, very sure of winning, also put down another four hundred dollars.

Matthewson's ten dogs were taken away, and Buck, who could feel the excitement in the air, was harnessed to the sled. Buck was, without question, a very fine animal—bright-eyed, intelligent, his thick coat shining with health. And he looked as strong as a horse.

One man went up to Thornton. "I'll buy him now," he said. "I'll give you eight hundred dollars for him."

Thornton shook his head and sat down on the snow next to Buck. He held Buck's head in his hands and spoke softly into his ear. "If you love me, Buck. If you love me."

"If you love me, Buck. If you love me."

47

Buck took Thornton's hand between his teeth, then let go, and Thornton stood up and stepped back.

"Ready, Buck," he said.

Buck pulled on the harness a little, getting ready.

"Right!" cried Thornton.

Buck pulled to the right, hard, stopped suddenly, and the ice under the sled began to break.

"Now, left!" called Thornton, and Buck pulled to the left, breaking more of the ice.

"Now, pull!"

Buck threw himself against his harness, and pulled. He

held his body low to the ground, his head down and forward, and his feet dug into the hard snow. Harder and harder he pulled. Suddenly, the sled moved an inch . . . two . . . three . . . and, little by little, it started to go forward across the snow. With each second it went a little faster, and Thornton ran behind, calling to Buck as he pulled the sled towards the end of the hundred yards. The watching men were shouting and throwing their hats in the air; Buck had won.

Then Thornton was on the snow next to Buck again, talking to him, and Buck had Thornton's hand in his teeth.

Buck had won.

7

The Call of the Wild

In five minutes Buck had made fourteen hundred dollars for Thornton and his friends. The money made it possible for them to travel east, where they wanted to look for a lost gold mine. Men said that this mine had more gold than any other mine in the north. Many had looked for it, and some had died looking for it. The only men who knew where it was were now dead.

Thornton, Pete, and Hans, with Buck and six other dogs, started off to the east in the spring. They traveled up the Stewart River and crossed the Mackenzie Mountains. They did not move quickly; the weather was good, and the men shot animals for food when they needed it. Sometimes they traveled for a week, and sometimes they stopped for a week and searched for gold in the ground. Sometimes they were hungry, and sometimes they had lots of food. They spent all the summer in the mountains, carrying everything they needed on their backs, sometimes making boats to go down rivers or across lakes.

In the autumn they came to a strange, flat country, with many lakes. They traveled on through the winter and met nobody, but once they found an old wooden house, with an old gun in it.

When the spring came, they found, not the lost mine, but a lake in a wide valley. Through the shallow water the gold showed like yellow butter, and here their search ended. There was gold worth thousands of dollars in the lake, and they worked every day, filling bag after bag with gold.

The dogs had nothing to do except watch the men and eat the food which the men shot for them. Buck spent many evenings sitting by the fire.

As he sat, he saw again his dream world, where the strange hairy man sat next to him. He also heard something calling him into the forest. Sometimes, in the middle of the day, he lifted his head and listened, and then he ran off into the forest.

One night he woke up and heard the call again, a long howl. He ran into the forest, following the sound, and came to an open place in the trees. And there, his nose pointing to the sky, sat a wolf.

There, his nose pointing to the sky, sat a wolf.

The wolf stopped howling, and Buck walked slowly towards him. The wolf ran, and Buck followed. After a time, the wolf stopped and waited, watching Buck, ready to attack. But Buck did not want to fight, and soon the wolf realized this, and the two animals became friendly. Then the wolf started to run again, and he clearly wanted Buck to follow him. They ran for hours through the forest, and Buck remembered again his dream world where he, and others like him, had run through a much older forest.

Then they stopped to drink, and Buck remembered John Thornton. He turned and started to run back. The wolf followed him, then stopped and howled, but Buck ran on and did not turn.

Thornton was eating dinner when Buck returned. Buck jumped all over him, and for two days never left his side. He followed him everywhere, watching him while he ate and while he slept. But after two days the call of the wild came again, and he remembered the forest and the wolf who had run beside him.

He started to sleep out in the forest at night, sometimes staying out for three or four days. Once he was away for a week, fishing and killing animals for food. He ate well, and he grew stronger, and quicker, and more alive. His golden-brown coat shone with health as he ran through the forest, learning its every secret, every smell, and every sound.

"He's the finest dog that I've ever seen," said Thornton to his friends one day as they watched Buck walking out of camp.

"There'll never be another dog like him," said Pete.

They saw him walking out of camp but they didn't see the change that happened when he was inside the forest. At once he became a thing of the wild, stepping softly and silently, a passing shadow among the trees.

In the autumn, Buck started to see moose in the forest. One day he met a group of about twenty. The largest was over six feet tall, and his antlers were seven feet across. When he saw Buck, he got very angry. For hours Buck followed the moose; he wanted the big one, but he wanted

When the moose saw Buck, he got very angry.

him alone. By the evening Buck had driven the big old moose away from the others, and then he began his attack. The animal weighed more than half a ton—he was big enough and strong enough to kill Buck in seconds.

Patiently, Buck followed him for four days, attacking and then jumping away. He gave him no peace, no time to eat or drink or rest, and slowly the moose became weaker. At the end of the fourth day Buck pulled the moose down and killed him. He stayed by the dead animal for a day and a half, eating, and then turned towards camp and John Thornton.

Three miles from the camp, he smelled something strange. Something was wrong. He started to run. After a few hundred yards he found the dead body of Blackie, with an arrow through his side. Then he found another sled-dog, dying, with an arrow in his neck.

He found Blackie with an arrow through his side.

Buck was near the camp now, and he could hear voices singing. Then he saw the body of Hans, lying on his face, with ten or fifteen arrows in his back. Buck was suddenly filled with a wild, burning anger.

The Yeehats were dancing around the camp, when they heard a deep and terrible growling. Buck came out of the trees faster than the north wind and threw himself on the Yeehats like a mad dog. He jumped at the first man and tore out his throat, killing him at once. He jumped onto a second, then a third man, going each time for the throat. The Yeehats could neither escape nor use their arrows.

Buck moved like a storm among them, tearing, biting, destroying, in a madness that he had never known before. Nothing could stop him, and soon the Yeehats were running, wild with fear, back to the forest. Buck followed for some time, then returned to the camp.

He found Pete, killed in his bed. He followed Thornton's smell to a deep pool, and found Skeet lying dead by the edge. Thornton's body was somewhere under the water.

He followed Thornton's smell to a deep pool.

All day Buck stayed by the pool or walked restlessly around the camp. But when the evening came, he heard new sounds from the forest; the wolves had come south for the winter, and were moving into Buck's valley. They came into the camp in the moonlight, and Buck stood silently, waiting for them. Suddenly, the bravest wolf jumped at Buck. In a second, Buck had bitten and then stood still again. The wolf was dead behind him. Three more wolves jumped at him and were killed.

Then the pack attacked in a crowd all at once. But not one of them could bring Buck down; he was too quick, too strong, too clever for them all. After half an hour the pack stopped attacking and moved away. Then one wolf moved forward slowly, in a friendly way; it was the wolf that Buck had met before in the forest. They touched noses. Then another wolf came forward to make friends, and another. Soon the pack was all around Buck, and the call of the wild was loud in Buck's ears. And when the wolves moved on, back into the forest, Buck ran with them, side by side.

That is perhaps the end of Buck's story. But after a few years, the Yeehats noticed that some of the wolves had golden-brown in their gray coats. They also talked of a Ghost Dog that ran at the head of the pack.

And sometimes men were found dead, killed by the teeth of a terrible animal. And each autumn, when the Yeehats follow the moose, there is one valley that they will not go into.

In the summers there is one visitor to that valley: a large, golden-brown wolf, larger than any other wolf. He walks alone around the lake where the yellow gold shines in the water and howls. But he is not always alone. In the long winter nights, he runs at the head of the wolf pack through the moonlight, calling into the night with them, singing a song from a younger world.

He runs at the head of the wolf pack through the moonlight.

GLOSSARY

attack to start fighting someone

bark (*n*) the short, sharp sound that a dog makes

bone one of the hard white parts inside an animal's or a person's body

fair a fair person is honest and divides things equally

growl to make a low angry noise in the throat

howl to make a loud, crying sound

law a rule made by people, or a law of nature, when the same thing always happens

lead (*v*) to go in front of another person (or dog)

leash to hold a dog on a long piece of rope

mad crazy; ill in the head

mine (*n*) a place where gold (or coal, etc.) is taken out of the ground

pack a number of animals traveling together

point (*v*) to hold something towards someone or something

rabies an illness that makes dogs crazy and then kills them

team a group of dogs working together

tear (past tense **tore**) to pull at something and make holes in it, or pull it to pieces

throat the front part of the neck

weak not strong

weigh to show how many pounds (ounces, etc.) something is

wolf a wild animal like a dog

The Call of the Wild

ACTIVITIES

Before Reading

1 **Read the story introduction on the first page of the book and the back cover. Are these sentences true (T) or false (F)?**

1 Buck had an easy life in California.
2 Buck runs away to the Yukon.
3 Men found gold in the Yukon in 1897.
4 Buck learns to pull a sled over the snow.
5 It is dangerous for a dog to fall down in a fight.
6 Buck learns slowly.
7 Buck becomes famous.

2 **What is going to happen in the story? Can you guess? For each sentence, circle Y (Yes) or N (No).**

1 Buck goes home to California. Y/N
2 Buck is killed by another dog. Y/N
3 Buck kills another dog. Y/N
4 Buck learns to hate all men. Y/N
5 Buck learns to love a man. Y/N
6 Buck runs away to live with the wolves in the forest. Y/N

While Reading

Read Chapter 1. Then answer these questions.

1 Where did Buck live until he was four years old?
2 Why did Manuel steal Buck from Mr. Miller?
3 How did the fat man make Buck obey him?
4 Who bought Buck?
5 How did Buck travel from Seattle to the north?
6 How many other dogs traveled with Buck?
7 What was the soft white thing that fell from the air?

Read Chapter 2. Choose the best question-word for these questions and then answer them.

How / What
1 . . . was Curly killed?
2 . . . did Buck learn to work in a harness?
3 . . . did Perrault have to take to Dawson City?
4 . . . did the dogs sleep in the snow?
5 . . . did Dave do to Buck when he pulled the wrong way?
6 . . . did the dogs eat?
7 . . . did Buck get more food?

Read Chapter 3. Are these sentences true (T) or false (F)? Rewrite the false ones with the correct information.

1 Spitz often tried to start a fight with Buck.
2 The Indian dogs fought because they were angry.
3 Perrault fell through the ice twelve times.
4 Buck had hard feet.
5 Dolly saved Buck when François tried to kill him.
6 Buck wanted to be lead-dog.
7 Spitz broke Buck's front legs.
8 When Spitz fell down, sixty dogs jumped on him.

Before you read Chapter 4, can you guess what happens? For each sentence, circle Y (Yes) or N (No).

1 Buck becomes the new leader. Y/N
2 The team works harder after Spitz dies. Y/N
3 François and Perrault sell Buck. Y/N
4 The dogs rest for two weeks after their next journey. Y/N
5 Someone shoots one of the dogs. Y/N
6 Buck runs away. Y/N

Read Chapter 5. Who said this, and to whom?

1 "How could we live without a tent?"
2 "Dogs are lazy and you have to whip them."
3 "Don't listen to that man."
4 "Why don't you pull hard?—then nobody will whip you."
5 "Only somebody very stupid would cross the White River here."
6 "I'm going to Dawson."

Read Chapter 6. Match these halves of sentences about Buck and Thornton.

1 Buck liked to take Thornton's hand in his mouth
2 Buck wanted to answer the call of the wild animals,
3 One day, Thornton told Buck to jump,
4 Buck attacked a man called Burton
5 When Thornton was thrown out of his boat into the river,
6 Buck pulled a sled with a thousand pounds on it

7 Buck jumped into the river with a rope and saved him.
8 to win money for Thornton.
9 but every time he went into the forest, he came back.
10 when Thornton talked to him.
11 because he saw Thornton in danger.
12 and Buck tried to jump three hundred feet down into the river.

Before you read Chapter 7, can you guess what happens? For each sentence, circle Y (Yes) or N (No).

1 Thornton and Buck travel east to look for gold. Y/N
2 A wild animal kills Thornton. Y/N
3 Indians kill Thornton. Y/N
4 Buck kills a wolf. Y/N
5 Thornton takes Buck back to California. Y/N
6 Buck joins a wolf pack. Y/N

After Reading

1 Use the chart to make sentences about Buck's life in the north.

Buck learned to . . .

wear a harness	when he wanted to drink.
dig a hole in the snow	because his feet were still soft.
eat his fish quickly	to pull a sled.
steal food	to sleep in.
break the ice on water holes	because it was in his blood.
fight like a wolf	before the other dogs stole it.
wear little shoes	because he was always hungry.

2 Match these halves of sentences to tell the story of how Buck killed Spitz. Use these words to join your sentences.

and / and / and then / and then / because / because / when / when

1 After that, he broke Spitz's right front leg,

2 Spitz hated Buck

3 The fight finished

4 He started to help the other dogs

5 After a few minutes, Buck bit Spitz's left front leg

6 Buck hated Spitz too,

7 Then one night Spitz caught a rabbit

8 Each time Buck attacked, Spitz moved

9 _____ the bone broke.

10 _____ the two dogs started to fight.

11 _____ he knew that Buck wanted to be lead-dog.

12 _____ Spitz disappeared under the waiting pack of dogs.

13 _____ bit him on the side.

14 _____ he made his final attack.

15 _____ Spitz punished them.

16 _____ he remembered him laughing when Curly died.

3 **What did you think about the characters in this story? Were they nice or nasty, clever or stupid? Did you feel sorry for any of them? Were they brave? Choose some characters, and complete some of these sentences.**

Buck / the fat man / Manuel / François / Perrault / Hal / Mercedes / John Thornton

1 I feel sorry for _____ because _____.

2 I think _____ was *right/wrong* to _____.

3 I think _____ did a very *bad/good/brave* thing when _____.

4 I think _____ did a very *clever/stupid/brave* thing when _____.

5 I think _____ was *stupider/nicer/nastier* than _____ because _____.

4 **This conversation between Hal and Mercedes is in the wrong order. Write it out in the correct order and put in the speakers' names. Hal speaks first (number 3).**

1 _____ "We all have to work. Life is like that in the north."

2 _____ "They won't fall off now. We've got much less luggage now that half the dog food is finished. We're not going to have enough to get us to Dawson."

3 _____ "You can't ride on the sled, Mercedes. The dogs are too tired."

4 _____ "I felt sorry for them, poor things."

5 _____ "But I'm tired too, and I'm your wife. You shouldn't make me work."

6 _____ "I wish we'd never come to the north. You don't know anything. You can't even pack the sled."

7 _____ "Well, you keep moving things, and then they fall off!"

8 _____ "If you felt really sorry for them, you'd get off the sled and walk!"

9 _____ "That's because you gave the dogs too much when we started!"

10 _____ "Well, I won't get off. You can't make me!"

5 **Do you agree (A) or disagree (D) with these sentences? Explain why.**

1 Manuel was wrong to use Buck to get money for his family.

2 It is wrong for people to make dogs work for them.

3 Buck was happier in the wild than with John Thornton.

6 **Use these words to fill in the gaps in this letter that Matthewson wrote to his wife.**

bar, below, break, dogs, dollars, frozen, harnessed, ice, lost, move, over, pounds, pull, pulled, sled, spoke, strong, teeth, win, yards

Dear Mary,

I am sorry that I cannot send you any more money yet, and all because of a dog! This is what happened. I was in a _____ with some men when we started to talk about _____. A man called Thornton said that his dog could pull a _____ with a thousand _____ on it, and I said that I would give him a thousand _____ if his dog could do that, but first the dog must _____ the sled out when it was _____ to the ice, and then _____ it a hundred yards _____ the snow. If Thornton _____, he was going to give me a thousand dollars. I was sure that I was going to _____, so in the end we made it fourteen hundred dollars. We _____ Buck, Thornton's dog, to my sled. He looked intelligent, healthy, and as _____ as a horse. But it was 50° _____ zero and the sled was frozen to the _____, so I thought that my money was safe. But there is something very strange about that man and his dog. Thornton _____ quietly to Buck; the dog took Thornton's hand between his _____, and then let go and started to pull. He _____ harder and harder, and suddenly, I saw the sled start to _____. That dog pulled it a hundred _____, and so I lost my money!

ABOUT THE AUTHOR

Jack London was born in 1876 in San Francisco, California. He came from a poor family and from a young age he hunted, stole, and worked at many different jobs—factory-worker, sailor, journalist—to make money to live. Like many men, he hurried to the Yukon in northern Canada to look for gold during the Klondike "gold rush" of 1897. He wrote his first book of stories *The Son of the Wolf* (1900), about his life there. He became well-known as a writer in 1903, after writing *The Call of the Wild*, which is also about the dangerous, frozen land of the north.

He wrote many other books. Some were adventure stories about sailors, hunters or fishermen, who fight both other men and the dangers of nature; and another famous story, *White Fang* (1906), was also about a dog. But London never forgot his difficult early years, and he felt deeply about poor people and the hard lives they had. He was a socialist all his life and, as well as his adventure stories, he wrote serious books about the class system and the need for social change.

Although he became rich and famous during his short life, Jack London was an unhappy man. He had a problem with alcohol and died when he was only forty, in 1916.

OXFORD BOOKWORMS LIBRARY

Classics • Crime & Mystery • Factfiles • Fantasy & Horror
Human Interest • Playscripts • Thriller & Adventure
True Stories • World Stories

The OXFORD BOOKWORMS LIBRARY provides enjoyable reading in English, with a wide range of classic and modern fiction, non-fiction, and plays. It includes original and adapted texts in seven carefully graded language stages which take learners from beginner to advanced level.

All Stage 1 titles, as well as over eighty other titles from Starter to Stage 6, are available as audio recordings. All Starters and many titles at Stages 1 to 4 are specially recommended for younger learners. Every Bookworm is illustrated, and Starters and Factfiles have full-color illustrations.

The OXFORD BOOKWORMS LIBRARY also offers extensive support. Each book contains an introduction to the story, notes about the author, a glossary, and activities. Additional resources include tests and worksheets, as well as answers for these and for the activities in the books. There is advice on running a class library, using audio recordings, and the many ways of using Oxford Bookworms in reading programs. Resource materials are available on the website <www.oup.com/elt/bookworms>.

The *Oxford Bookworms Collection* is a series for advanced learners. It consists of volumes of short stories by well-known authors, both classic and modern. Texts are not abridged or adapted in any way, but carefully selected to be accessible to the advanced student.

You can find details and a full list of titles in the *Oxford Bookworms Library Catalog* and *Oxford English Language Teaching Catalogs*, and on the website <www.oup.com/elt/bookworms>.

A Christmas Carol

CHARLES DICKENS

Retold by Clare West

Christmas is humbug, Scrooge says—just a time when you find yourself a year older and not a penny richer. The only thing that matters to Scrooge is business, and making money.

But on Christmas Eve three spirits come to visit him. They take him traveling on the wings of the night to see the shadows of Christmas past, present, and future—and Scrooge learns a lesson that he will never forget.

The Secret Garden

FRANCES HODGSON BURNETT

Retold by Clare West

Little Mary Lennox is a bad-tempered, disagreeable child. When her parents die in India, she is sent back to England to live with her uncle in a big, lonely old house.

There is nothing to do all day except walk in the gardens—and watch the robin flying over the high walls of the secret garden . . . which has been locked for ten years. And no one has the key.

Frankenstein

MARY SHELLEY

Retold by Patrick Nobes

Victor Frankenstein thinks he has found the secret of life. He takes parts from dead people and builds a new "man." But this monster is so big and frightening that everyone runs away from him—even Frankenstein himself!

The monster is like an enormous baby who needs love. But nobody gives him love, and soon he learns to hate. And, because he is so strong, the next thing he learns is how to kill . . .

A Tale of Two Cities

CHARLES DICKENS

Retold by Ralph Mowat

"The Marquis lay there, like stone, with a knife pushed into his heart. On his chest lay a piece of paper, with the words: *Drive him fast to the grave. This is from JACQUES.*"

The French Revolution brings terror and death to many people. But even in these troubled times people can still love and be kind. They can be generous, true-hearted . . . and brave.

Little Women

LOUISA MAY ALCOTT

Retold by John Escott

When Christmas comes for the four March girls, there is no money for expensive presents, and they give away their Christmas breakfast to a poor family. But there are no happier girls in America than Meg, Jo, Beth, and Amy. They miss their father, of course, who is away at the Civil War, but they try hard to be good so that he will be proud of his "little women" when he comes home.

This heart-warming story of family life has been popular for more than a hundred years.

Dr. Jekyll and Mr. Hyde

ROBERT LOUIS STEVENSON

Retold by Rosemary Border

You are walking through the streets of London. It is getting dark, and you want to get home quickly. You enter a narrow side-street. Everything is quiet, but as you pass the door of a large windowless building, you hear a key turning in the lock. A man comes out and looks at you. You have never seen him before, but you realize immediately that he hates you. You are shocked to discover, also, that you hate him.

Who is this man that everybody hates? And why is he coming out of the laboratory of the very respectable Dr. Jekyll?